DATE			

SUCCESSFUL

CRABBING

*This fine fossil specimen was found by George H. Moss, Jr.,
on a beach in Sea Bright, New Jersey, after a violent storm in
1962. Personnel of New York's American Museum of Natural
History identified it as an arthropod fossil belonging to the
genus* Callinectes *and coming from early tertiary sediments.
It was estimated to be between 63 and 75 million years old.*

SUCCESSFUL

CRABBING

Ernest J. Cottrell
Frank L. Mellaci
John B. Cottrell

International Marine Publishing Company
Camden, Maine

CONTENTS

ACKNOWLEDGMENTS

The authors wish to express their gratitude to Dr. Robert K. Tucker, National Marine Fisheries scientist, whose knowledge, cooperation, and guidance helped better acquaint us with many fascinating aspects of the blue crab; to Mr. W. A. Van Engle, Senior Marine Scientist, Virginia Institute of Marine Science, who supplied helpful direction and guidance; to Mr. D. W. Bennett, Conservation Director of the American Littoral Society, for his encouragement and cooperation; and to Barbara Cottrell, director of the library in Fair Haven, New Jersey, for pointing out the need for this book. Also, to librarian Mabel Trafford of the National Marine Fisheries Service, whose research assistance brought to light many original scientific papers, texts, and journals that were extremely helpful in the preparation of the first paragraphs of this book.

PREFACE

Although the blue crab has considerable economic value, and has been caught and eaten by many people, very little has been known of its life history, even in scientific circles, until relatively recently. Through the untiring efforts of public and private marine laboratories, enough facts have been assembled so that it is now possible to piece together the fascinating story of the blue crab. Much of this information does not exist elsewhere, except in highly technical form. We have attempted to tell this story in an interesting, easy-to-follow manner, generally avoiding technical terms. However, it has been necessary to use some technical terms, and these are explained in the Glossary, along with additional relevant words. The Bibliography lists the literature that will be helpful to those wishing to study the blue crab in greater detail.

PART I

LIFE STORY
OF THE BLUE CRAB

Callinectes sapidus, which can be translated freely as *savory graceful swimmer,* is the correct name for the blue crab. *Callinectes sapidus* belongs to the family Portunidae, or swimming crabs; the two rear legs are flattened and are used as fins in swimming. Crabs that do not have the rear pair of legs flattened are unable to swim and move only by crawling. All crabs of the Portunidae family, in which the abdomen or apron of the male crab is ⊥-shaped, belong to the genus *Callinectes.* The species *Callinectes sapidus,* the edible blue crab, is a familiar sight along the entire east coast and estuaries of the United States, and it is the most widely distributed of all the species of *Callinectes.* The blue crab is found as far north as Nova Scotia and as far south as northern Argentina. It is also found on the Atlantic coast of France and in the North Sea near Denmark and the Netherlands.

It is believed that the blue crab was not present in the Mediterranean before 1940, but since then it has been introduced accidentally by small specimens being discharged with water from the ballast tanks of oceangoing vessels. After becoming established in the western Mediterranean, the blue crab spread to the countries bordering the Mediterranean on the north, then east into Egyptian waters in the Nile.

The blue crab is found in sheltered coves and bays in the brackish water of estuaries and mouths of rivers, especially around muddy shores and bottoms. The blue crab can be recognized by the large, sharp spine on each side of its top shell, which distinguishes it from many other crabs. The top shell is grayish-, bluish-, or brownish-green; its shades vary diurnally. The legs and claws are white with splotches of bright blue, and they may also have tiny splotches of red. The female may have larger splotches of red, especially on the claws. Blue crabs perform a limited migration; after mating, the males remain in the upper estuary waters, while the females migrate toward the ocean. After hatching and passing through the larval stages and entering the first crab stage, the offspring migrate to the upper-estuary waters of lower salinity, where they remain until mature. Both males and females spend the winter months in deeper waters in semi-hibernation, rarely eating or moving. Their life span, according to scientific estimates, may be as long as five years. Most of the time the blue crab has a hard shell and is called a hard crab; periodically it must molt (shed its old shell) to facilitate growth. Just before shedding it is called a shedder, and upon shedding it becomes a soft crab.

Chapter 1

BIRTH AND EARLY LIFE

The Parents

Our story of the blue crab starts with the mating of a mature male and female. The exact time of mating varies in accordance with environmental factors, such as salt content (salinity) of the water, season, light, temperature, and availability of food. It also varies with geographical location. In the estuaries and bays bordering the east coast of the United States, mating occurs from the early weeks of spring through late October, with the last two weeks of August and the month of September marking the peak of the mating season. Farther south, on the Gulf coast, the mating season extends from December to October. After mating, the male remains in the upper estuary, where the salinity is approximately five to 15 parts per thousand (ppt); the female, carrying the spermatozoa of the male, migrates toward deeper water with a salinity of almost 30 ppt and remains there, although some go out in the ocean and may venture as far as the continental shelf. The salinity of open ocean water ranges from 30 to 34 ppt. The presence of great numbers of females each fall in the waters at the lower reaches of estuaries and bays near the ocean gives evidence of this migration. The incubation period of the eggs is 15 to 18 days in the warm summer waters. Incubation is slowed by the cooling of the waters in the fall, and it is practically stopped during cold weather. If the mating occurred in the waning weeks of summer, the female will spend the winter months resting peacefully in a state of semi-hibernation, becoming active in the spring when the water temperatures rise to around 50 or 60 degrees Fahrenheit and the environmental factors necessary for the incubation and hatching of the eggs are present. The developing eggs form a struc-ture that resembles a sponge on the abdomen of the female; hence, the egg-laden female is called a sponge crab (Fig. 1-1).

The Birth

At the completion of the incubation period, the eggs begin to hatch. This probably will occur near the mouth of the estuary in the place selected by the sponge crab, and it may take a few days for all the eggs to hatch. It is estimated that there are between 1,500,000 and 2,000,000 eggs in a good-sized, healthy sponge. If the appropriate environmental factors are present, most of the eggs will hatch, liberating the tiny crab larvae, which measure approximately .01 inch in diameter. The crab larva are in the first zoeal stage and bear no resemblance to their parents as they leave the eggs to enter the plankton. They are now faced with a perilous existence, competing with the other denizens of the plankton in the struggle for survival. The hazards are so extreme that if 2,000,000 eggs hatched, fewer than 50 crabs, or approximately .0025 percent, could be expected to reach maturity.

The female has the capability of storing some of the male spermatozoa from the mating. After

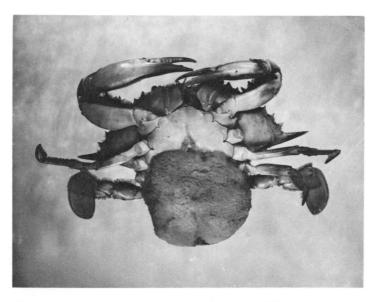

Figure 1-1. Sponge crab. Courtesy of the Virginia Institute of Marine Science, Gloucester Point, Virginia.

the eggs from the initial sponge have hatched, and after a brief rest period, the now-unencumbered female may release some of the stored spermatozoa to fertilize a second group of eggs. If this occurs, a new sponge will form and the entire process is repeated while the female remains near the mouth of the estuary. It is possible for the female then to produce a third, and probably final, group of fertilized eggs.

In the Plankton

Plankton comes from a Greek word meaning "wandering." This is an appropriate name: the microscopic flora and fauna that form the major portion of the plankton are transported wherever the currents and tides dictate. The newly liberated crab larvae will spend nearly two months among the myriad of microscopic plants and animals in the plankton, none of which seem to resemble their parents. The plants and animals are known as phytoplankton and zooplankton, respectively. The phytoplankton consist of desmids and diatoms, which, through photosynthesis, convert minerals and carbon dioxide from the sea into carbohydrate foodstuffs. The zooplankton include one-celled animals, as well as the young of crabs, barnacles, lobsters, and fish. The zooplankton lack the ability to produce their own food and must eat the plants or eat other animals that have fed on the plants to obtain the necessary nutrition for growth and development. This predator-prey relationship forms the basis for a multitude of food chains in which every animal becomes an active participant (Fig. 1-2). Materials pass from the plants through a series

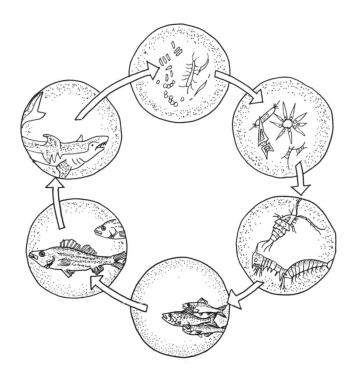

Figure 1-2. The food chain. Starting with bacteria and fungi at the top and proceeding clockwise, energy is transferred to phytoplankton, then to zooplankton, then to progressively larger animals until, with the death and decomposition of an animal, the cycle starts over. Drawing by Joan Marsh.

of animals, until an animal dies. Then the action of bacteria and fungi decomposes the dead animal and releases the simple chemical substances that will be utilized again by the phytoplankton to form nutrients, and the cycle is repeated. Animals in a food chain are smaller and more numerous in the earlier stages, and larger and less numerous in the later stages. National and private marine laboratories, knowing that fish and other species of marine life depend entirely on plankton for food, are currently exploring the feasibility of utilizing this protein-rich substance as a supplemental or alternate source of food if our present sources of food should dwindle; this, as well as their experiments with the aquaculture of larger species, may someday make the dream of farming the sea a reality.

The Zoeal Stages

The larva progresses through seven zoeal stages in about a month, molting between stages and growing approximately 50 percent larger with each molt. In the first zoeal stage (Fig. 1-3), the larva is microscopic. Seen through a low-power microscope, it is not at all like the adult. The body is almost cylindrical, with large, dark eyes. The eyes will become slightly stalked in the second zoeal stage. There is a sharp spine on the dorsal portion of the body. The abdomen is long and round and tapers to a forked tail. A sharp spine is seen on the head. Two pairs of antennae are quite noticeable, as are four pairs of leglike appendages; the true legs do not appear until later. Although in the zoeal stages the larvae are mobile, they are usually at the mercy of the tides and currents. They move by rapid movements of the abdomen in a forward direction toward the front or ventral side of the body. Seven zoeal stages have been observed in the laboratory, although they may not occur in exactly the same way under natural conditions.

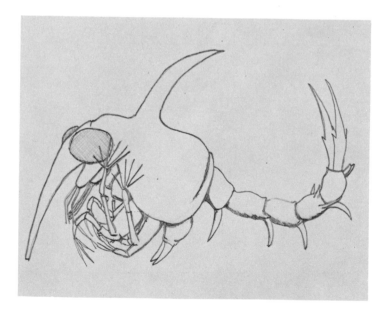

Figure 1-3. Crab larva in a zoeal stage. Drawing by Joan Friedman.

The Megalops Stage

Following the last zoeal stage, the larva molts and metamorphoses into the megalops stage (Fig. 1-4). It has grown approximately 50 percent larger with this molt and is now almost .15 inch in diameter. In the megalops stage there is a marked resemblance to the adult crab. The body is flattened laterally in a dorsal-to-ventral perspective, with the abdomen shorter and wider than it was in the zoea,

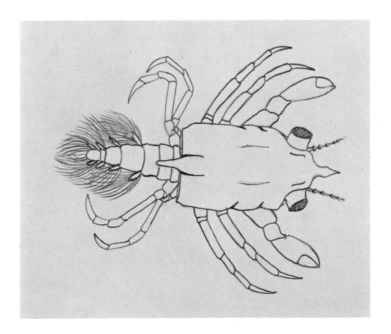

Figure 1-4. Crab larva in the megalops stage. Drawing by Joan Friedman.

but not yet curled up against the ventral portion of the body. The leglike appendages have developed into legs, but the rear pair have yet to develop the paddlelike appearance, and they will remain pointed until the succeeding molt into the first crab stage. The megalops may drift with tides and currents, as in the zoeal stages, but now it also has the ability to walk on the bottom. These dual methods of mobility increase the range of distribution and increase the percentage of individuals that will eventually reach maturity. The duration of the megalops stage is from six to 20 days, completing the period spent in the plankton. The larva then molts and metamorphoses into the first crab stage.

The Young Blue Crab

With the molt from the megalops stage, each larva has metamorphosed into a tiny replica of the adult crab and has grown to almost .22 inch in diameter. When the young crabs are about four months old, they begin their migration to the upper estuary waters of lower salinity. For many, this migration is not completed before the onset of winter. The inhibiting effect of colder weather causes the young crabs to reduce their activity, temporarily discontinuing their migration. When spring comes and the water becomes warmer, the young crabs become active again and continue their migration to the upper estuaries. It is here, in the warm, food-laden waters of the upper estuary, that the crabs reach maturity approximately 13 to 14 months from the time of hatching. The crabs have molted approximately eight times in the larval stages and 12 to 18 times in the crab stage before reaching maturity. The male may molt one or two times more than the female, a fact that would account for his being somewhat larger than the female. The average size of the adult blue crab is about seven inches point to point, although some have been reported up to 12 inches. The crabs are now sexually mature and able to mate. During August and September we find considerable numbers of mating pairs (doublers), giving confirmation that it is the height of the mating season. Following copulation, which occurs but once in her life, the female begins her migration toward the ocean. The males remain in the waters of the upper estuary, wintering in the deeper channels and becoming active again in the spring. The females, as did their mothers, seek the higher-salinity water that will be required by their spawn. They will probably spend the winter in deep water near the mouth of the estuary. When longer sunlight hours of spring raise water temperatures, the eggs of the females hatch, contributing to the survival of the species. It is the offspring of these and succeeding generations of crabs that will provide hours of fun and relaxation for the human generations of tomorrow.

Chapter 2

THE ADULT BLUE CRAB

Hard Crabs

The adult crab, in its hard-shell form, is very active and has remarkable strength and dexterity in its claws. It can swim rapidly, and frequently may travel a few miles at a time, swimming near the surface and with the tide. It prefers a muddy bottom and will push itself backward into the mud with just the eyes protruding, watching for food and hiding from enemies. It is predacious and opportunistic, feeding upon almost any small animal or fish that it can catch, as well as upon oysters, plant material, and carrion. It is pugnacious and a fearless fighter, using its claws in a ferocious manner. Each of the two claws has a specialized use (Fig. 2-1). One claw has smaller, sharper teeth and is used for biting and cutting, as well as for striking out at prey. The other claw has larger, rounded teeth and is used for crushing and for holding food while the cutting claw removes small pieces and conveys them to the mouth. Males can be distinguished from females by the shape of the abdomen (apron) on

the underside; the male always has a narrow apron (Fig. 2-2), the immature female has a wide triangular apron (Fig. 2-3), and the mature female has a rounded apron (Fig. 2-4).

Shedders

Before it is time to shed, the crab must grow a soft shell under the old hard shell. This will protect the crab after leaving the old shell and will eventually harden and become the new hard shell. The shedder looks very much like an ordinary hard crab, except that its apron is darker and has a purplish

Figure 2-1. Front view of hard crab. Note cutting claw on right (crab's left) and crushing claw on left.

Figure 2-2. Bottom view of male crab.

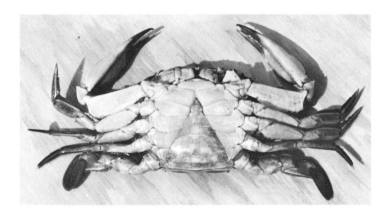

Figure 2-3. Bottom view of female crab. The triangular apron indicates an immature female. The darkness of the apron indicates that it is also a shedder.

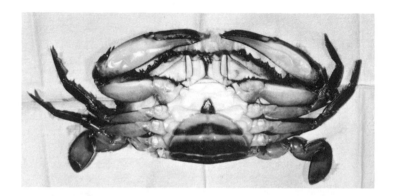

Figure 2-4. Bottom view of female crab. The rounded apron indicates a mature female.

look. The female crab shown in Figure 2-3 is also a shedder, as indicated by the dark apron. Each adult female shedder will usually pair up with an adult male a day or two before she is due to shed. The two crabs together are called doublers. The male carries the female in an upright position under his body. When it is time for her to shed, he releases her and stands by while she sheds, then clasps her again under his body, this time holding her upside down. In this position, with the abdomens of the two crabs together, mating is accomplished. Several hours later, after mating is completed, the female resumes the upright position but remains under the male for protection while she is relatively helpless as a soft crab. As her shell gradually hardens over the next day or so, she becomes a paperback, then a tinback, and then a hard crab once more. Shortly after this, the crabs part and go their separate ways. The female will work her way closer to the ocean before the eggs she is carrying are due to hatch, because she is seeking the higher-salinity water the new offspring will require. Male shedders and young female shedders shed alone on the bottom.

Soft Crabs

The shedder crab instinctively looks for a safe place when it is time to shed. In the soft state, the crab is considered a delightful meal by just about every sea creature that happens along. So the shedder seeks a shallow place near the edge of the water, from a few inches to over a foot deep, and usually sheds when the tide is going out. The shedding takes only a few minutes (Figs. 2-5 through 2-8); the top shell of the crab separates at the back and lifts up and the crab slowly backs out, pulling its claws, legs, and swimming fins out a little at a time. When the crab is completely out, it lies behind the old shell and rests—tired, weak, and wrinkled. It has already grown larger than the shell it has just left and continues to grow until all the wrinkles are gone. At this point, it is quite a lot larger than the old shell and is not quite so weak. If unmolested, the new soft crab will probably lie behind the old shell and rest, becoming stronger rapidly, and it

Figure 2-5. Shedder crab starting to shed but still moving, apparently looking for the right place. The shell has separated at the back. At this stage the crab is called a buster.

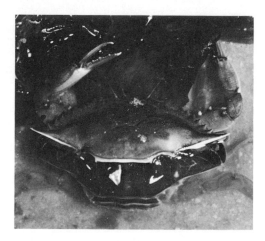

Figure 2-6. The shedder starting to back out. Notice how the spine on each side of the top shell is folded under the old shell.

Figure 2-7. The shedder is almost out.

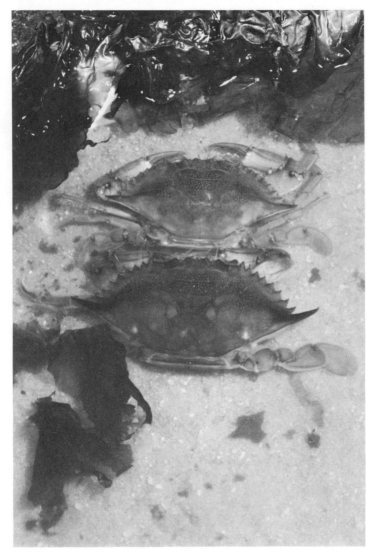

Figure 2-8. New soft crab resting behind old shell.

will soon leave the shallow spot to slip away into deeper water. The soft shell will slowly harden over the next day or so; the crab will become a paperback, then a tinback, and finally a hard crab once more. If a predator comes along, the soft crab will lift its claws in a threatening manner, hoping to bluff the predator. If the predator is fooled, it will leave the soft crab alone and look for other prey. However, the crab is not safe until its shell is completely hard again.

PART II

CRABBING FOR FUN

Chapters 3 and 4 describe the various methods of catching crabs and provide detailed instructions for each method. If these instructions are followed in an area where crabs exist, the crabber is certain to be rewarded with many hours of interesting fun and some delicious morsels to take home and cook. Certain methods tend to overlap; for instance, we would almost never catch a soft crab when using a baited hand line or a crab trap, but it would be possible to catch a soft crab while looking around the pilings of docks and bridges for hard crabs. And, when looking for soft crabs from a boat or while walking, we would be likely to catch hard crabs also. When seining, we would be likely to catch hard crabs and soft crabs, as well as many other little animals and fish. In fact, one of the delightful things about seining is being able to look forward to the many surprises we find in the net.

Whichever method is used, keep only the larger crabs. Any that are smaller than approximately five inches point to point should be returned to the water, especially the females, whose function, besides carrying the eggs during incubation, is to find a suitable environment that will ensure the proliferation of the species.

As most of us well know, our estuaries are a prime breeding ground for a wide variety of birds, fish, and crustaceans. More than 25 of our nation's most important commercial species of fish, mollusks, and crustaceans spend part, if not all, of their lives in an estuary. These estuaries supply a lifeline of nutrients. Our intrusion into the marine domain has been intensive and devastating, and until we can remedy this and dispose of the wastes of our so-called civilized world, the burden on our estuaries will continue to be severe. By practicing some simple conservation measures, such as being careful not to pollute and returning the young or immature of not only the blue crab but all marine specimens, the strain on our marine-animal population will be greatly reduced.

Chapter 3

HOW TO CATCH HARD CRABS

Hard crabs are usually caught by one of four methods. The most common, and probably the most fun, is using a baited hand line. Crab traps may also be used. Other methods are to look for crabs clinging to pilings around docks and bridges, or to use a seine.

Caution: The hard crab's claws are very powerful, and its pinch is painful. A crab pinch will frequently cut through the skin to cause bleeding, and it may be a very deep cut. If it is necessary to pick up a hard crab with the hands, be sure to hold the crab by one or both of the swimming fins (Fig. 3-1), and be careful not to let your fingers extend too far under the crab, because it can reach back a good distance under its shell.

The question of which bait to use for catching crabs has long been argued. Different kinds of fish, as well as pieces of meat or chicken, seem to be the favorites. Some people say that the bait works best when it is spoiled and smelly, but this is doubtful. In our experience, the best bait of all is spearing or live killies (killifish) strung on a circular wire. If you are squeamish about stringing live killies on a wire, get some fresh dead ones and string them. The second-best bait is fish heads and the remains of filleted fish from the local fish market.

*Figure 3-1. Correct method of holding hard crab. (*Note: *Children normally should wear life preservers when in a boat.)*

This bait is very good and has the added advantage of usually being free. The third-best bait is frozen menhaden (mossbunkers), which are usually sold at rowboat rental places.

To make a good, serviceable hand line, attach the bait to a short piece of string or fishing line. The line should be long enough to reach the bottom, plus a little more to allow the crabber to try slightly different locations from the same vantage point. A weight (sinker) should be added and should be just heavy enough to overcome the buoyancy of the bait in the prevailing current and take it to the bottom. Avoid using sinkers that are heavier than necessary; a light line is more sensitive, and therefore it makes it easier to tell when a crab is biting.

To make a better hand line, you will need a piece of stiff stainless-steel wire, such as piano wire or heavy fishing leader, about 20 inches long, a sinker with a connecting link, a swivel, and a piece of plastic tubing three or four inches long. Using Figure 3-2 as a guide, attach one end of the stiff wire to one side of the swivel, then attach the connecting link with the sinker to the same point. Next, put the piece of plastic tubing on the wire and push it up near the swivel. The plastic tubing should be slightly larger than the wire, so that when the loose end of the wire is pushed in, it will fit snugly. Finally, tie the line to the other side of the swivel, and the hand line is complete. (Choose your line length and sinker weight as described for the simpler hand line.)

This stiff wire hand line works well with all kinds of bait; it is also very easy to remove the bait when one is finished crabbing for the day. If you are using spearing or killies, put them on the wire one after the other by inserting the loose end of the stiff wire in the fish's mouth and pushing the wire in until it comes out lower down on its body. When the wire is almost full, push the loose end into the plastic tubing and the baiting is completed (Fig. 3-3). To put pieces of larger fish on the line, use an ice pick or an awl to make two holes in the piece of fish. Pass the loose end of the stiff wire through one hole, then back through the other, then push the loose end of the stiff wire into the plastic tubing (Fig. 3-4).

Figure 3-2. Completed hand line.

Figure 3-3. Hand line baited with spearing.

Figure 3-4. Hand line baited with piece of mossbunker.

31

The crabber can hold the hand line and feel when a crab comes and touches the bait. The line is then gently lifted a few inches, and if it feels a little heavier than it did before, it means a crab is on. Some crabs really pull on the line, some try to take the bait sideways, and others just hang on and enjoy the free meal. As long as the crab stays on, the line should be pulled up slowly to the surface while the net is held in readiness. This is the critical moment (Fig. 3-5). If the crab becomes alarmed, it

Figure 3-5. The critical moment. The crab is near the surface.

Figure 3-6. The critical moment is past. The crab is in the net.

will let go and disappear. If this should happen, drop the line back down and the crab may come back to the bait. Some crabbers like to put the net down in the water before the crab becomes visible and then maneuver the bait and crab over the net, while others bring the bait and crab close to the surface, and then, with a swift motion, scoop up the crab.

A trotline is a variation of the hand line and is used to catch large numbers of crabs. The trotline consists of a long, heavy line to which short, lighter lines are attached at intervals, usually six to 10 feet apart. The long, heavy line is fixed at each end, usually to an anchor and a buoy. The short lines are baited in much the same manner as the hand line. The crabber pulls his boat along by means of the heavy line and checks each short line in turn, netting any crabs that may be at the bait. This method is popular on the Chesapeake Bay, an area that probably produces more blue crabs than anywhere else on earth. The trotline may be used by recreational crabbers on a small scale, or it may be used by commercial crabbers on a larger scale. Some commercial crabbers have developed it to a high degree, and service trotlines hundreds of feet long.

Crab Traps

The crab trap is a wire basket in which bait is attached (Fig. 3-7). The crab trap is fastened to a

Figure 3-7. Crab trap baited with remains of filleted bluefish.

Figure 3-8. Crab trap with crab inside.

heavy line in such a manner that when the line is slack the sides open, and when the line is pulled tight the sides close. When the crab trap is lowered to the bottom and the line becomes slack, the sides open and a crab may go inside to get at the bait. At intervals, the crabber gives a fast pull on the line, which closes the trap sides, and then, more leisurely, he pulls the trap to the surface. This method does not require as much finesse as the hand-line method; a fast, hard pull to close the trap quickly is used instead of the gentle lifting.

Commercial crabbers use another type of trap. It is a larger cage-type box that is baited and put in the water with a line attached to a buoy. It functions in much the same way as a lobster pot, having funnels that permit easy access but make it difficult for the crab, once inside, to find the way out. The crabber usually sets a number of these pots, leaving them set several hours before returning to pull them up and remove the catch.

Pilings

Searching around pilings usually works best later in the season, when the crabs are doubling up. A large male hard crab and a smaller female shedder crab will generally make up the pair (Fig. 3-9), and they seem to have a fondness for clinging to pilings. A boat may be used to go around the pilings and look for crabs, although some people use a long-handled net and walk along the top of a bridge or dock, peering down at the pilings. When a crab or a pair is spotted, the crabber must approach cautiously and be very quick and skillful with the net. The slightest mistake will alarm the quarry and it will disappear. Doublers find it a little harder to move fast and therefore are a little easier to catch. If a pair of

Figure 3-9. Doublers in net. Male hard crab with female shedder.

37

doublers is caught, the male hard crab should be put in the basket with the other hard crabs and the female (bottom) crab of the pair should be inspected. If it is a soft crab, keep it separate from the hard crabs; if it is not soft, the chances are that it is a shedder. If the apron is dark and purplish instead of white (Fig. 2-3), it is almost certain to be a shedder, and it should be kept separate from both hard crabs and soft crabs; and at the earliest opportunity it should be placed in a live box and allowed to shed and become a soft crab. The live box, often a makeshift wood-and-wire contraption, holds the crabs in water until they are removed and cooked.

Chapter 4

HOW TO CATCH SOFT CRABS

It's necessary to change tactics to catch soft crabs. Instead of using bait to attract the crabs or looking around pilings in deep water, look around the edges of coves and in other shallow areas.

The ideal time to catch soft crabs is after the tide has been going out for a while, and the areas the crabs are likely to have used for shedding are just becoming visible. The water must be clear enough to see the bottom at least a few feet from the edge. A boat may be used, or the crabber may walk along the edge or across any shallow areas. A third method, which works best when the tide is partly out and which does not require clear water, is seining.

Crabbing with a Boat

The rowboat is traditional for crabbing, but use any boat that allows you to stand well up in the bow and see the area in front of the boat while poling or paddling along. Generally, a small, low boat is best and easiest to handle; small so that you can maneuver it easily and low so that you can avoid being affected too much if it happens to be windy.

It is best to go against the tide, because any muddy water that might be stirred up will go to the rear of the boat, and the crabbing area will stay clear. Also, if a crab is spotted, it is easier to stop the boat without alarming it. Avoid letting your shadow fall on the crab.

With the net ready at hand, paddle or pole along slowly. Look carefully at any little depressions on the bottom and around any obstacles, such as a small rock, an old tin can, or any place the crab about to shed might select for protection. What you are looking for is what appears to be a medium-sized crab, slightly brownish, with a larger crab, slightly bluish, directly behind (Fig. 4-1). This is actually a soft crab lying behind the shell he has just vacated. This is the traditional pattern, but don't pass up other crabs, especially if they look bluish and are moving slowly. The latter could be soft crabs that have left the old shell. When you see the crab, approach it carefully. If it is near an obstacle, it may be necessary to use the oar as well as the net; place the net carefully on one side of the crab and the oar on the other, then wiggle the oar to alarm the crab and make it run into the net. At this point it is futile to give instructions: you must rely

Figure 4-1. Soft crab resting next to vacated shell (top).

on your own native cunning. If you catch any doublers (Fig. 4-2), be sure to separate them as described in Chapter 3.

Walking

The crabber may walk along the edge, carrying a net and a small basket. Where there are large shallow areas, the crabber can tow a floating basket in an innertube. The basket should have three compartments if you intend to keep the hard crabs. If not, the basket need only have two

Figure 4-2. Two pairs of doublers in net. The two pairs were near each other and the crabber was able to capture both. Bottom pair is a male hard crab with a female shedder and top pair is a male hard crab with a female soft crab.

compartments: one for soft crabs and one for shedders. Be sure to wear something on your feet to protect them from sharp shells, broken glass, and other hazards.

As with the boat, it is best to go against the tide; in fact, it is even more important, because walking usually stirs up a great deal of muddy water. If you see a crab, avoid frightening it with your shadow.

The method of finding and catching crabs is the same as that used with a boat. It may be useful to carry a small stick about the size of a walking stick, since you won't have an oar handy if the crab is near an obstacle.

Seining

Seining is a good way to catch soft crabs and hard crabs, as well as bait such as killies and spearing. In fact, with a seine you can walk along in shallow water and catch just about anything, and this makes it extremely interesting. The seine is a long, fine-mesh net with floats along the top and sinkers along the bottom. The seine shown in Figure 4-3 is 24 feet long and about average length. The longer the seine, the wider the sweep you can make, and the more productive it will be. Two people are required, and they must hold the poles almost vertical, with the lower end just sliding along the bottom. The faster the seine is moved, the better.

Seining requires quite a lot of energy, so don't try it unless you are in good health and have been fairly active. Pick a likely shallow area and make a sweep that winds up on the beach. The most enjoyable part of seining is looking through the net after each haul (Fig. 4-4). Many kinds of delightful surprises await you. Have fun; but, after you pick out what you want to keep, remember to return the rest to the water.

Figure 4-3. Seining.

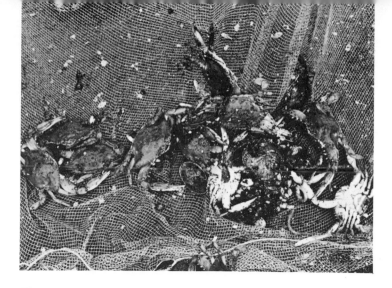

Figure 4-4. A fair haul.

PART III

COOKING AND
EATING CRABS

Many good cookbooks contain excellent recipes for cooking crabs and these are recommended to the reader, as well as the few recipes herein, all of which are useful, with one or two being unusual. It seems, however, that there is a lack of information on cleaning crabs, so we have attempted to give detailed instructions for this task.

Chapter 5

PREPARING HARD CRABS

The Crab Meat

Crab meat is commercially graded as lump meat, flake meat, and claw meat.

Lump meat, sometimes called backfin meat, is the muscle tissue that moves the swimming fins. It is located in the two rear body compartments, next to the swimming fins, and is considered the best.

Flake meat is the muscle tissue that moves the walking legs. It is located in the six body compartments next to the walking legs and is considered second best.

Claw meat is the muscle tissue that moves and controls the claws. It is located in the claws and in the two front body compartments next to the claws. Claw meat is considered third best (but still delicious).

Cooking Hard Crabs

Because of the blue crabs' ornery disposition, augmented by their lightning-fast claws, it is recommended that the crabs be transferred from the carrying basket into the kitchen sink, so that hot water can be run over them before they are cooked. This procedure removes any debris clinging to their shells and partially anesthetizes them, making them easier to handle and less susceptible to pain in the early stages of cooking. Hard crabs may be boiled or steamed with spices. After cooking, the crab meat is picked from the shell and used in crab-meat recipes (Fig. 5-1).

Figure 5-1. Bottom view of cooked hard crab with portions of shell removed to show location of meat in body compartments and claws.

BOILED CRABS

Use a large pot one third full of water, and proceed as follows. Add a pinch of salt, some sliced celery stalks, and a dash of vinegar to enhance the flavor. Bring to a boil. Drop the crabs into the boiling water and let them boil approximately 15 minutes. By this time the crabs will have turned red. Pour off the water and let the crabs cool.

SPICY STEAMED CRABS

Use a large pot with a rack raised at least two inches from the bottom and proceed as follows. For each dozen crabs, mix 3 tablespoons of salt and 2½ tablespoons of seasoning, such as Old Bay Seasoning. Add equal quantities of vinegar and water to the pot to a level just below the rack. Place the crabs in the pot in layers, with the mixture of salt and seasoning sprinkled between each layer. Cover, bring to a boil, and steam 15 to 20 minutes. Remove the crabs and allow to cool.

Picking Hard Crabs

Picking consists of removing the edible portions of the crab after cooking. Proceed as follows:

51

(1) Break off the legs and the claws, discarding the legs. Crack the claws with a nutcracker or mallet and remove the meat.

(2) Use a thin knife or other utensil to loosen and remove the top shell (Fig. 5-2).

(3) Remove and discard the feathery gills (Fig. 5-3).

(4) Remove the mouth parts and rinse out the contents of the stomach (area behind the mouth). Break the body in two lengthwise, and pick out the meat from the body compartments (Fig. 5-4).

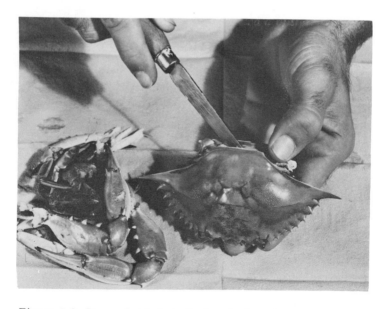

Figure 5-2. Removing top shell of cooked crab.

Figure 5-3. Removing gills.

Figure 5-4. Picking out meat from body compartments.

53

Crab-Meat Recipes

The following recipes are prepared with cooked crab meat removed from the shell.

SPICED CRAB CAKES

2 slices bread with crust removed
small amount of milk
1 lb. crab meat
1 tsp. seasoning, such as Old Bay Seasoning
¼ tsp. salt
1 tbsp. mayonnaise
1 tbsp. Worcestershire sauce
1 tbsp. chopped parsley
1 tbsp. baking powder
1 egg, beaten

Break the bread into small pieces and moisten with the milk. Mix together all the ingredients and shape into cakes. Fry quickly until brown.

CRAB-MEAT CRÊPES WITH MORNAY SAUCE

1 lb. flaked crab meat
1 pint Mornay sauce
salt
white pepper
12 crêpes
3 oz. grated Gruyère cheese

Check the crab meat carefully to be sure all membrane material has been removed. Mix the crab meat with enough Mornay sauce to form a moist mixture. Season with salt and pepper. Divide the mixture evenly among the crêpes and roll the crêpes tightly. Arrange the rolled crêpes in a buttered baking dish. Pour the rest of the Mornay sauce over the rolled crêpes and sprinkle with the grated Gruyère cheese. Place in a 350 degree F. oven until the top is a light golden brown.

Recipes with Whole Crabs

TOMATO SAUCE WITH CRABS

2 or more live hard crabs
¼ cup olive oil
1 medium onion, chopped
1 carrot, grated
1 celery stalk, finely chopped
2 garlic cloves, minced
½ tsp. oregano
½ tsp. basil
¼ tsp. black pepper
1 large can Italian tomatoes
1 6-oz. can tomato paste

Heat oil; add carrot, onion, and celery. Sauté until onion and celery are transparent, add garlic, and sauté briefly. Stir in remaining ingredients except tomato paste, bring to boil, and simmer over medium-low heat. Dilute tomato paste with 2½ cups of warm water, then add to sauce. Continue cooking sauce, stirring frequently, until it thickens, 75 to 90 minutes. While sauce cooks, split live crabs top to bottom with a cleaver. Remove and discard top shell, gills, eyes, mouth parts, and stomach. Crack claws and rinse crabs. Add crabs to sauce about 20 minutes before it is done.

CRAB CIOPPINO

2 or more live hard crabs
3 lbs. assorted fish, cleaned and cut into 2-inch
  pieces
1 dozen shrimp with shells
1 dozen clams in shells
1 carrot, chopped
1 onion, chopped
1 green pepper, chopped
1 celery stalk, chopped
¼ cup olive oil
3 tbsp. butter or margarine
1 cup dry white wine
2 cups whole-pack tomatoes, chopped
2 tbsp. parsley, chopped
2 garlic cloves, minced
½ tsp. oregano
salt
black pepper

Heat oil in heavy saucepan; add carrot, onion,
celery, and green pepper. Sauté until just soft, then
add garlic and sauté one minute longer. Add
tomatoes, 1½ cups water, wine, parsley, oregano,
salt to taste, and a dash of pepper. Cover, bring to
a boil, and let simmer 35 minutes. Split the live
crabs top to bottom with a cleaver. Remove and

57

discard the top shell, gills, eyes, mouth parts, and stomach. Crack the claws and rinse the crabs thoroughly. Rinse the fish and shrimp and place in the sauce along with the crabs. Cover and simmer 25 minutes longer. Add scrubbed clams to the sauce; cioppino is ready as soon as clam shells have opened. Serve in soup plates with crusty Italian bread accompanied by your favorite wine.

Chapter 6

PREPARING SOFT CRABS

Cleaning Soft Crabs

Cleaning soft crabs consists of removing the inedible portions before cooking. The remainder is cooked and eaten in its entirety. Proceed as follows:

(1) Pull the apron and associated structures away from the body. With sharp scissors, cut off the apron at the body line (Fig. 6-1).

(2) Cut off the mouth parts just behind the eyestalks (Fig. 6-2).

(3) Pull up the pointed end on one side of the top shell and cut off the gills, which lie underneath. Repeat for the other side (Fig. 6-3).

(4) Insert finger and remove the stomach from behind the mouth area, then rinse crab thoroughly (Fig. 6-4).

Cooking Soft Crabs

After the soft crabs have been cleaned, they may be sautéed, deep-fried, or baked *(recipes, page 62)*.

59

Figure 6-1. Removing apron of soft crab.

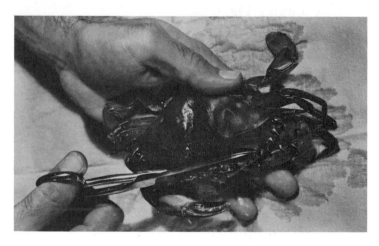

Figure 6-2. Removing eye and mouth area.

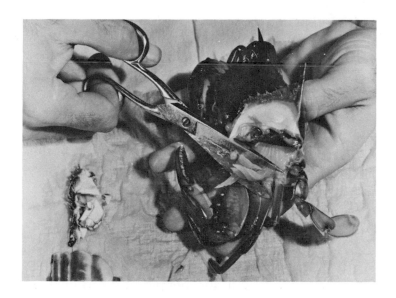

Figure 6-3. Removing gills.

Figure 6-4. Removing stomach.

61

SAUTÉED CRABS

Wash crabs thoroughly and remove excess water. Season crabs with salt and pepper and dip in flour. Heat 6 tablespoons of butter and 2 tablespoons of oil in a skillet. Place the crabs in the hot skillet and cook until they are delicately browned and crisp. This should take about 4 minutes on each side. Sprinkle each crab with chopped parsley and serve on a piece of toast, or in a sandwich.

DEEP-FRIED CRABS

Wash crabs thoroughly and remove excess water. Season crabs with salt and pepper and dip in flour. Add 2 tablespoons of water to 1 egg and beat lightly. Dip crabs in egg, then in bread crumbs, corn meal, or corn-flake crumbs. Fry in deep fat (400 degrees F.) approximately 4 minutes, then remove and drain on paper towels. Sprinkle with chopped parsley and serve.

BAKED CRABS

To bake soft crabs, prepare as for deep-frying, then place the crabs in a greased baking pan. Put a little butter on each crab and place the pan in a hot oven, about 400 degrees F., for approximately 8 minutes. Remove from oven, sprinkle with chopped parsley, and serve.

BIBLIOGRAPHY

Arnold, Augusta Foote. *The Sea-Beach at Ebb-tide.* New York: The Century Co., 1903.

Blake, Sidney Fay. The Pleistocene Fauna of Wailes Bluff and Langleys Bluff, Md. *Smithsonian Miscellaneous Collections,* vol. 121, no. 12, p. 32, 1953.

Buchsbaum, Ralph. *Animals without Backbones.* Chicago: The University of Chicago Press, 1948.

Cargo, David G. "The Blue Crab in Maryland Estuarine Waters." *Maryland Tidewater News,* vol. 12, no. 2, pp. 1-2, 1955.

Carson, Rachel L. *"Food From the Sea; Fish and Shellfish of New England."* U. S. Department of the Interior, Conservation Bulletin no. 33, p. 74, 1943.

The Edge of the Sea. New York: Houghton-Mifflin Co., 1955.

The Sea Around Us. New York: Golden Press, 1958.

Carter, G. S. *A General Zoology of the Inverte-*

brates. New York: Macmillan Co., 1940.

Churchill, Edward P., Jr. "Life History of the Blue Crab." *Bulletin of U.S. Bureau of Fisheries for 1917-1918,* vol. 36, pp. 91-128, 1921.
"The Zoeal Stages of the Blue Crab, *Callinectes sapidus.*" Chesapeake Biological Laboratory, Solomon, Md. Pub. no. 49, p. 26, 1942.

Coker, R. E. *This Great and Wide Sea.* Chapel Hill, N.C.: University of North Carolina Press, 1947.

Costlow, J. D., Jr. "Larval Development." *American Institute of Biological Sciences Bulletin,* vol. 13, no. 5, pp. 63-65, 1963.
"The Effect of Salinity and Temperature on Survival and Metamorphosis of Megalops of the Blue Crab *Callinectes sapidus.*" Helgolaender Wissenschaftliche Meeresuntersuchungen, vol. 15, no. 1, pp. 84-97, 1967.
"Variability in Larval Stages of the Blue Crab, *Callinectes sapidus.*" *Biological Bulletin* (Woods Hole), vol. 128, no. 1, pp. 58-66, 1965.

Costlow, J. D., Jr., and C. G. Bookhout. "The Larval Development of *Callinectes sapidus* Rathbun Reared in the Laboratory." *Biological Bulletin* (Woods Hole), vol. 116, no. 3, pp. 373-96, 1959.

Costlow, J. D., Jr., C. G. Bookhout, and George H. Rees. "Preliminary Note on the Complete Larval Development of *Callinectes sapidus* Rathbun Under Laboratory Conditions." *Limnology and*

Oceanography, vol. 4, no. 2, pp. 222-23, 1959.

Fishing News International. "Invasion. Desperation as Blue Crabs Swamp Nile Delta." *Fishing News International*, vol. 4, no. 1, pp. 56-57, 1965.

Holthuis, Lipke B. "An Early Account of the Natural History of Delaware." *Estuarine Bulletin,* vol. 3, pp. 4-9, 1958.

Holthuis, Lipke B., and E. Gottlieb. "The Occurrence of the American Blue Crab, *Callinectes sapidus* Rathbun, in Israeli Waters." *Bulletin of the Research Council of Israel,* vol. 5B, no. 2, pp. 154-56, 1955.

Rathbun, Mary J. "The Genus *Callinectes.*" *Proceedings of the U.S. National Museum*, vol. 18, pp. 349-75, 1896.

Fossil Crustacea of the Atlantic and Gulf Coastal Plain. Geological Society of America, Special Paper no. 2, pp. 1-160, 1935.

U. S. Fish and Wildlife Service. "The Blue Crab, *Callinectes sapidus.*" Fishery Leaflet no. 282, p. 3, 1948.

U. S. National Museum. "The Cancroid Crabs of America of the Families Euryalidae, Portunidae, Atelecyclidae, Cancridae, and Xanthidae." Bulletin 152, p. 609, 1930.

W. A. Van Engle. "The Blue Crab and Its Fishery in Chesapeake Bay." *Commercial Fisheries Review*, vol. 20, no. 6, pp. 6-17, 1958.

Villee, C. A. *Biology*. Philadelphia: W. B.

Saunders Co., 1967.

Williams, Austin B.   "A Ten-Year Study of Mero-
plankton in North Carolina Estuaries: Annual
Occurrence of Some Brachyuran Development
Stages." *Chesapeake Science,* vol. 12, no. 2,
p. 53, 1971.
"Marine Decapod Crustaceans of the Carolinas."
U. S. Fish and Wildlife Service, *Fishery Bul-
letin,* vol. 65, no. 1, pp. 1-298, 1965.
"The Swimming Crabs of the Genus *Callinectes*
(Decapoda: Portunidae)." U. S. Fish and Wild-
life Service, *Fishery Bulletin,* vol. 72, no. 3,
pp. 687-792, 1974.

Wilson, D. P.   *Life of the Shore and Shallow Sea.*
London: Collins, 1935.

Wolff, T.   "Occurrence of Two East American
Species of Crabs in European Waters." *Nature*
(London), vol. 174, no. 4421, pp. 188-89, 1954.

GLOSSARY

ABDOMEN: The body region posterior to the thorax. In crabs, this is the area covered by the apron.

ADAPTATION: The process by which an organism becomes better suited or adjusted to its environment.

ALGAE: The simplest plants, both single-celled and many-celled, containing chlorophyll.

ANTENNAE: Projecting sense organs on the heads of invertebrates.

APPENDAGE: An outgrowth of the body of an animal, such as claws, legs, or antennae.

APRON: Crab's distinctive abdominal area by which taxonomic and sexual characteristics are determined.

AQUATIC: Living in water, fresh or salt.

ARTHROPODS: Largest phylum; characterized by a segmented body, segmented appendages, and a chitinous exoskeleton; examples are crabs, lobsters, and insects.

BACTERIA: A group of microscopic, one-celled protists. Important in the decomposition of organic material.

BIOLOGICAL FACTOR: An influence resulting from biological as opposed to physical, chemical, and climatic conditions.

BIOSPHERE: The area in which life is possible on a planet.

BUSTER: Colloquial name for a crab that has begun, but not completed, molting (shedding).

CARAPACE: The hard upper shell of the crab.

CARRION: Dead and decaying meat.

CHELIPEDS: First pair of legs in most decapod crustaceans; specialized as claws for seizing and crushing.

CHEMICAL FACTOR: An influence resulting from chemical as opposed to biological, physical, and climatic conditions.

CHITIN: An important constituent of the exoskeleton.

CHLOROPHYLL: Green pigments that produce food in plants.

CLASS: A major subdivision of a phylum.

CLIMATIC FACTOR: An influence resulting from climatic as opposed to biological, physical, and chemical conditions.

COMMUNITY: In biology, a group of interdependent organisms in a particular environment.

CONSUMER: A plant or animal in a food chain that

cannot produce its own food and must eat other plants or animals.

CONTINENTAL SHELF: That portion of the sea bottom between the tidal zone and a depth of about 100 fathoms.

COPEPODA: Microscopic crustacean of the plankton.

CRUSTACEA: One of the eight classes in the phylum Arthropoda; includes copepods, crayfish, lobsters, crabs, and barnacles.

DECAPODA: Order of Malacostracan crustacea; includes crayfish, lobsters, and shrimp.

DECAY: The reduction of plant and animal substances into simple compounds by bacteria and fungi.

DECOMPOSERS: Collectively, those organisms (bacteria and fungi) in an ecosystem that convert dead organic materials into inorganic materials.

DESMID: Any of various green, unicellular algae of the family Desmidiaceae, sometimes forming chainlike colonies.

D.D.T.: The insecticide dichloro-diphenyl-trichlorethane.

DIATOM: A one-celled microscopic alga in the class Bacillareaceae, with siliceous walls.

DIFFERENTIATION: The development of a cell, organ, or immature organism into a mature organism; development of different kinds of organisms in the course of evolution.

DINOFLAGELLATE: A motile organism in the class Dinophyceae of the algae; great abundance of some forms is called red tide and may cause death of many fish and other marine organisms.

DISPERSION: The pattern of distribution of individuals of a population.

DISTRIBUTION: The geographic range (continuous or discontinuous) of a taxon at any one time.

DIURNAL: Pertaining to or occurring in a day or daily.

DORSAL: Relating to an animal's back side.

ECOLOGY: The study of the relationship of living things to their environment.

ECOSYSTEM: Collectively, all organisms in a community plus the associated environmental factors.

ENVIRONMENT: All the surrounding physical conditions in which an organism or cell lives, including available energy and living and nonliving material.

ENVIRONMENTAL FACTORS: The biological, physical, chemical, and climatic conditions to which an organism is subjected.

ESTUARY: An area where the tide meets the river current; an arm of the sea at the lower end of a river.

EXOSKELETON: Any invertebrate skeleton that forms the outermost covering of the body, giving it support and permanent shape.

EXTINCT: No longer in existence.

FAUNA: The sum total of the kinds of animals in an area at one time.

FERTILIZATION: Union of the male and female reproductive cells that gives rise to a fertile egg.

FLORA: The sum total of the kinds of plants in an area at one time.

FLUCTUATE: To vary irregularly; undergo alternating changes or repeated variations.

FOOD CHAIN: The transfer of energy as organisms feed on one another.

FOSSIL: Preserved remains in the earth's rock of a plant or animal of an earlier age.

FREE-SWIMMING: Moving about or capable of moving about in the water.

GENUS: A group of closely related species.

GILLS: Aquatic respiratory organ; thin-walled tissues in fish and other water animals that permit absorption of dissolved oxygen from surrounding water.

HABITAT: The specific place where a plant or animal lives; used in a more restrictive sense than environment.

HIBERNATION: State or period of inactivity applicable to a wintering animal.

INSTINCT: A simple to complex invariable behavior pattern usually assumed to be an innate pattern of successive reflexes not based upon previous experience.

71

INVERTEBRATES: Animals without backbones.

LARVAL FORM: The early form of some animals that is unlike their parents; the animal must pass through a metamorphosis before assuming the form of the parents.

LIFE CYCLE: Series of morphological changes and activities of an organism from the time of egg fertilization until death.

MALACOSTRACA: One of the subclasses in the class Crustacea; includes lobsters, crabs, crayfish, and shrimp.

MARINE: Living in or related to salt water.

MEGALOPS: The larval stage of marine crabs that precedes the first true crab stage.

METAMORPHOSIS: A marked change in the form or structure of an animal during development.

MIGRATION: Periodic change in location; seasonal movement from one region to another.

MOLT: Periodic shedding of the exoskeleton to permit an increase in size.

PAPERBACK: Colloquial name for a crab that, after being soft, is just starting to become hard again so that the top shell feels like stiff paper.

PHOTOSYNTHESIS: The synthesis of carbohydrates from carbon dioxide and water by chlorophyll, using light as energy and producing oxygen as a by-product.

PHYLUM: One of the principal divisions in the animal kingdom.

PHYTOPLANKTON: Collectively, all those microscopic plants suspended in the water of aquatic habitats; includes algae and some fungi.

PLANKTON: Microscopic plants and animals that exist near the surface of the water, including the young of larger organisms.

PREDATION: The capturing of prey to sustain life.

PREDATOR: Any animal that kills and consumes another animal.

PRODUCERS: The autotrophs in an environment. The plants that convert inorganic elements into organic compounds.

SALINITY: The salt content of water, expressed in parts of dissolved salts per 1,000 parts of water.

SCAVENGER: An animal that eats animal wastes or dead bodies of animals not killed by itself.

SEAWEED: An alga, usually large, growing in seas, bays, and estuaries. Seaweeds are held stationary by structures called holdfasts.

SHELLFISH: Common category that includes shelled mollusks and crustaceans, especially those used as human food.

SPECIES: Classification that designates a single kind; group of organisms that are capable of interbreeding and reproductively isolated from other groups.

SPONGE CRAB: Female crab laden with developing eggs.

TAXON: Any taxonomic category, such as species, genus, or class.

TAXONOMY: The branch of biology that groups and names living things.

THORAX: The central portion of the body between the head and abdomen.

TINBACK: Colloquial name for a crab that, after being soft, is almost hard again so that the top shell feels like thin metal.

TOLERANCE: An organism's ability to withstand varying environmental conditions.

VENTRAL: Relating to an animal's underside.

ZOEA: One of the larval stages of the blue crab.

ZOOPLANKTON: Collectively, all those animals suspended in the water of an aquatic habitat that are not independent of water movements; most such organisms are microscopic and commonly include protozoans and small crustaceans.

INDEX

SUCCESSFUL CRABBING